THE CORONAVIRUS 03/04/2020

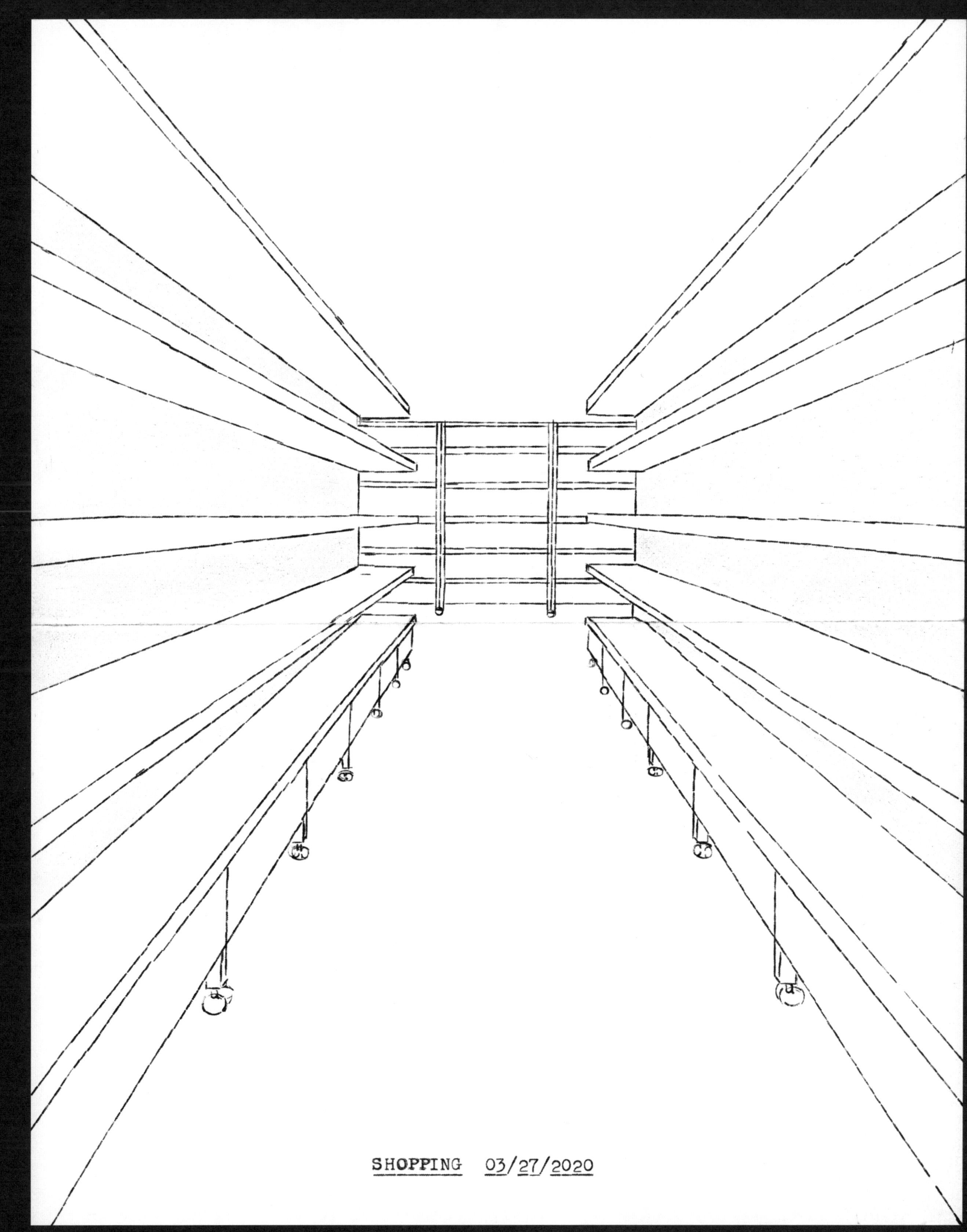

SHOPPING 03/27/2020

GRANDMA ON ZOOM 09/06/2020

<u>BEST FRIEND'S NEW BABY</u> 09/09/2020

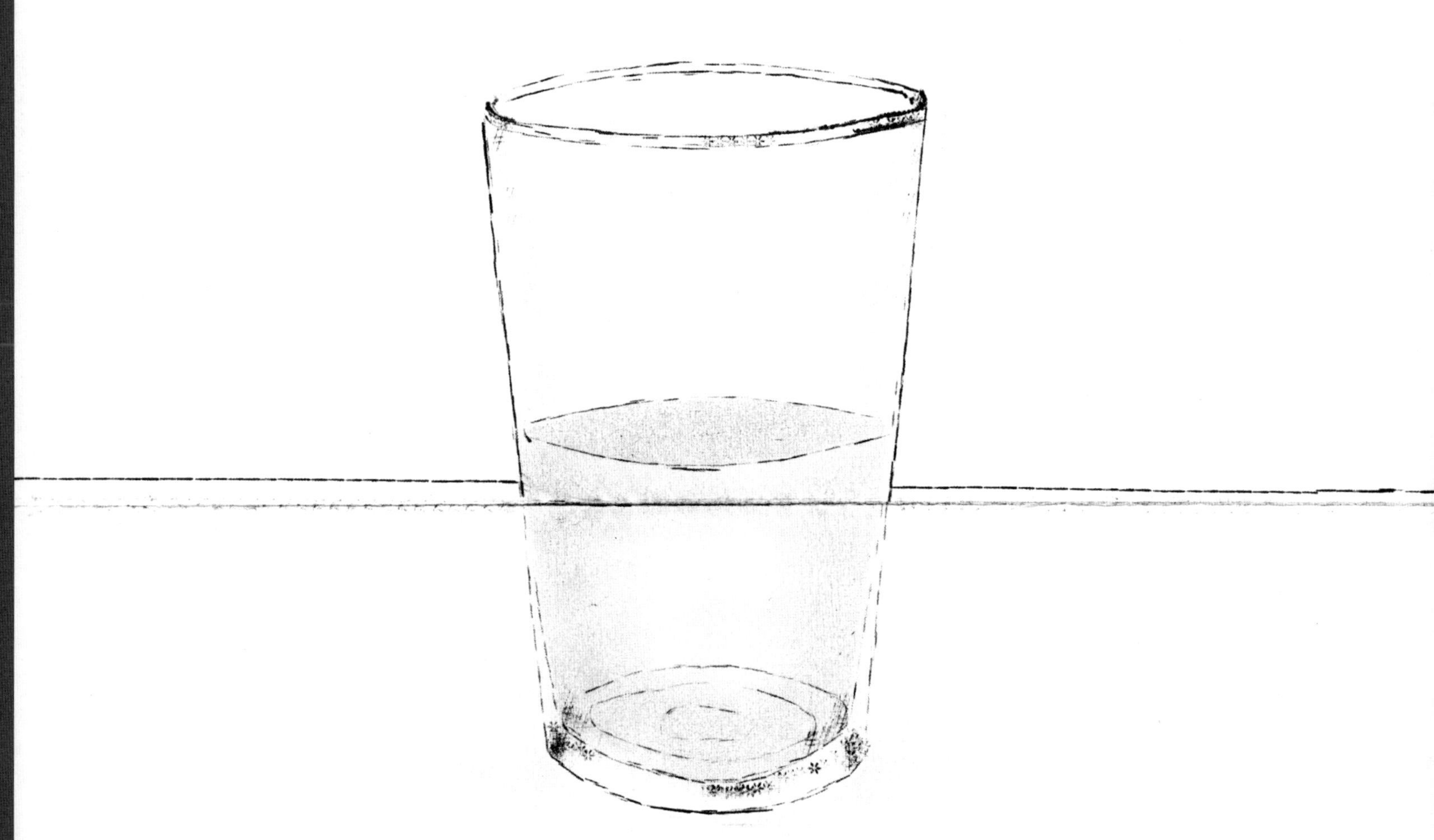

GLASS HALF FULL OF TEARS 09/12/20-20

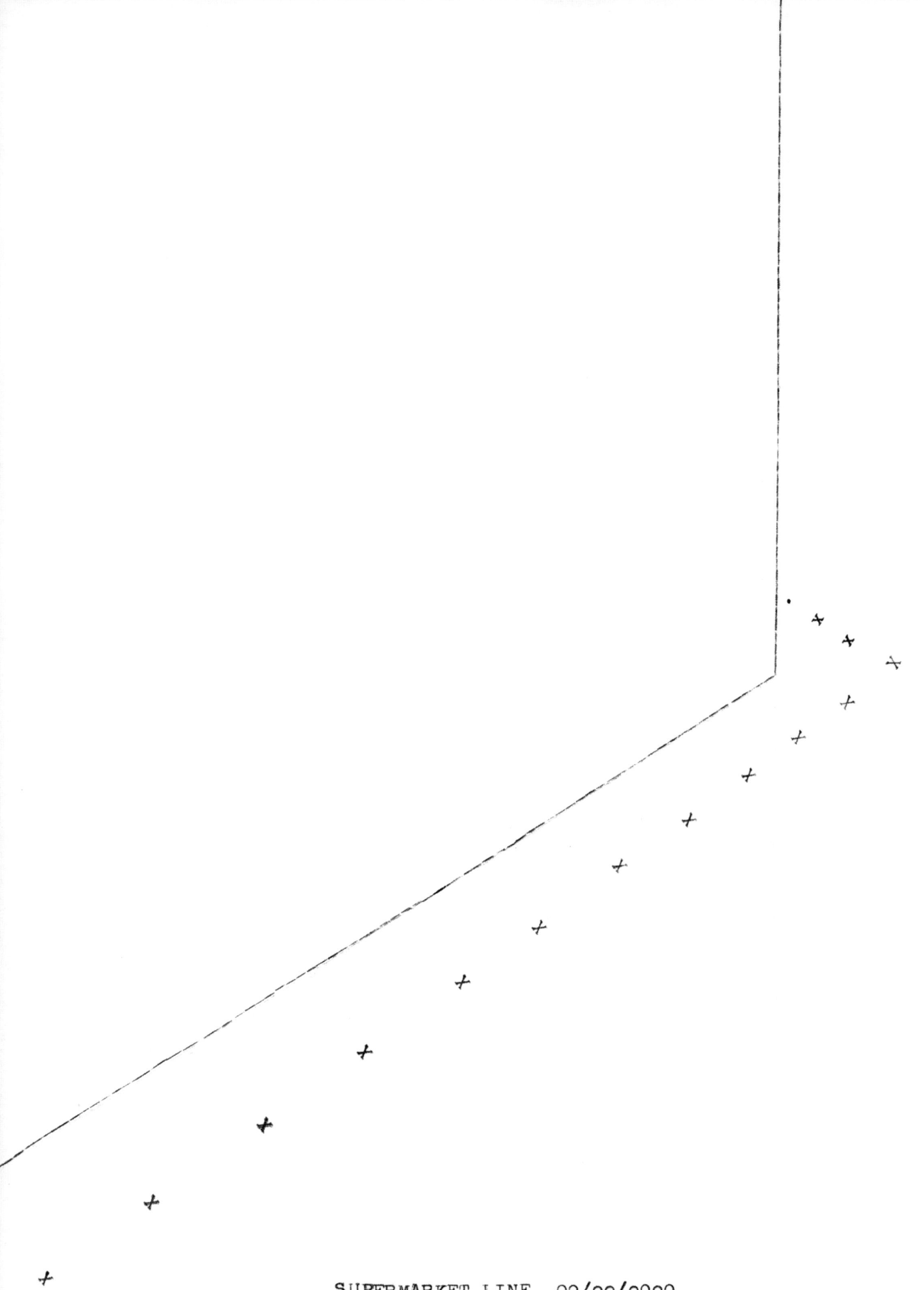

SUPERMARKET LINE 09/22/2020

AIR PURIFIER 09/28/2020

BOOKS IN QUARANTINE 09/30/2020

PANIC BOUGHT SPAGHETTI 10/01/2020

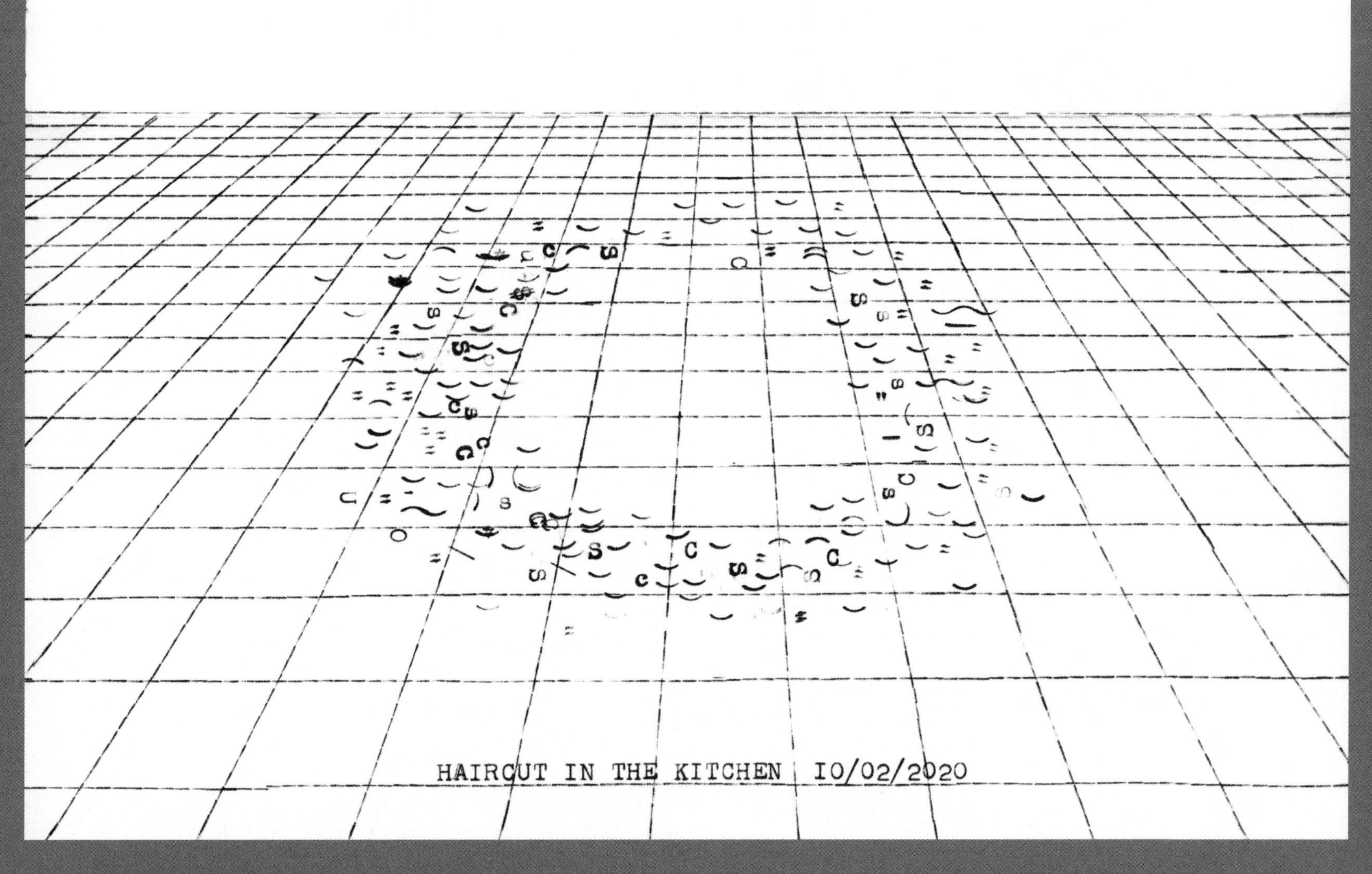

HAIRCUT IN THE KITCHEN 10/02/2020

PRETENDING TO WORK FROM THE HOSPITAL 10/04/2020

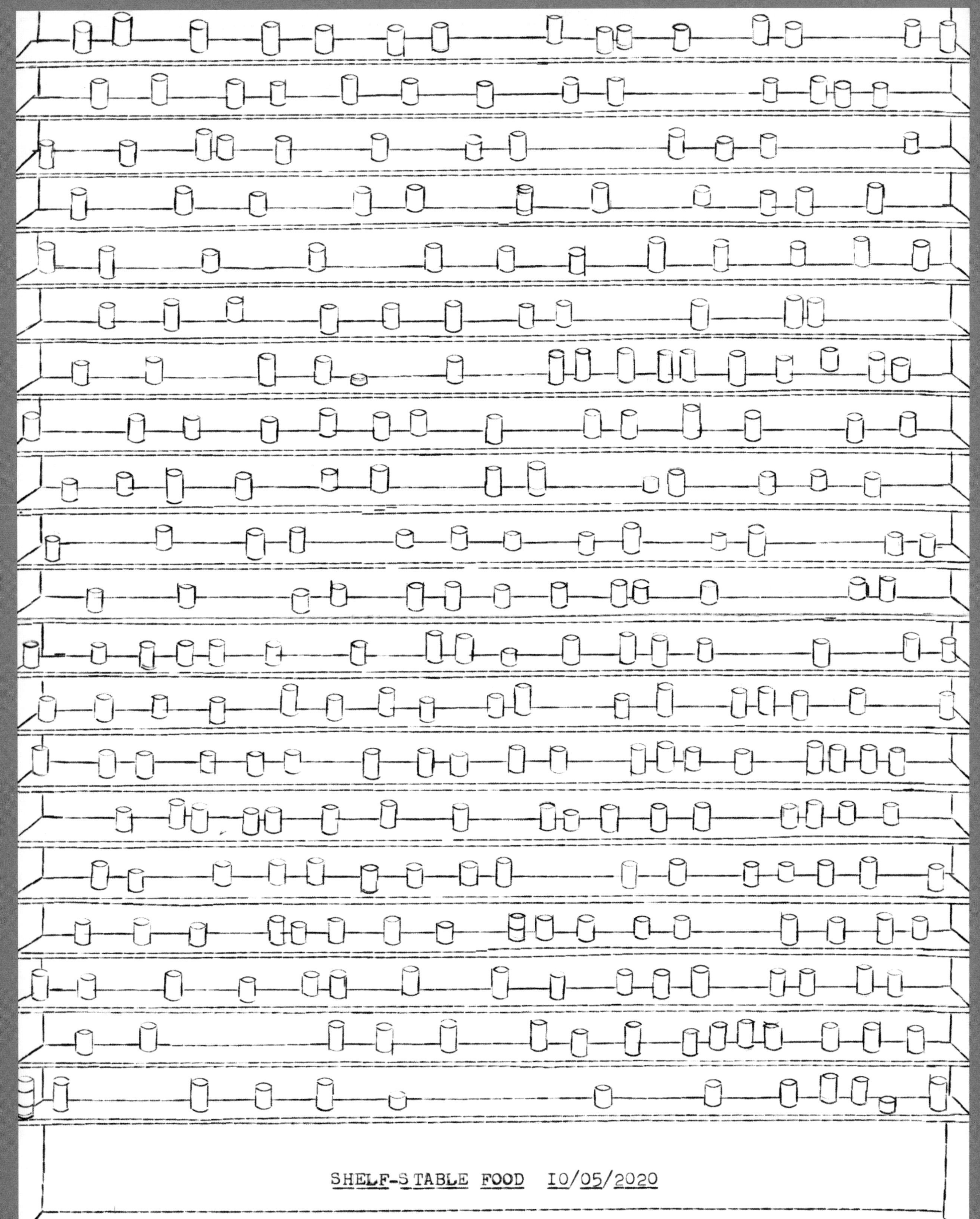
SHELF-STABLE FOOD 10/05/2020

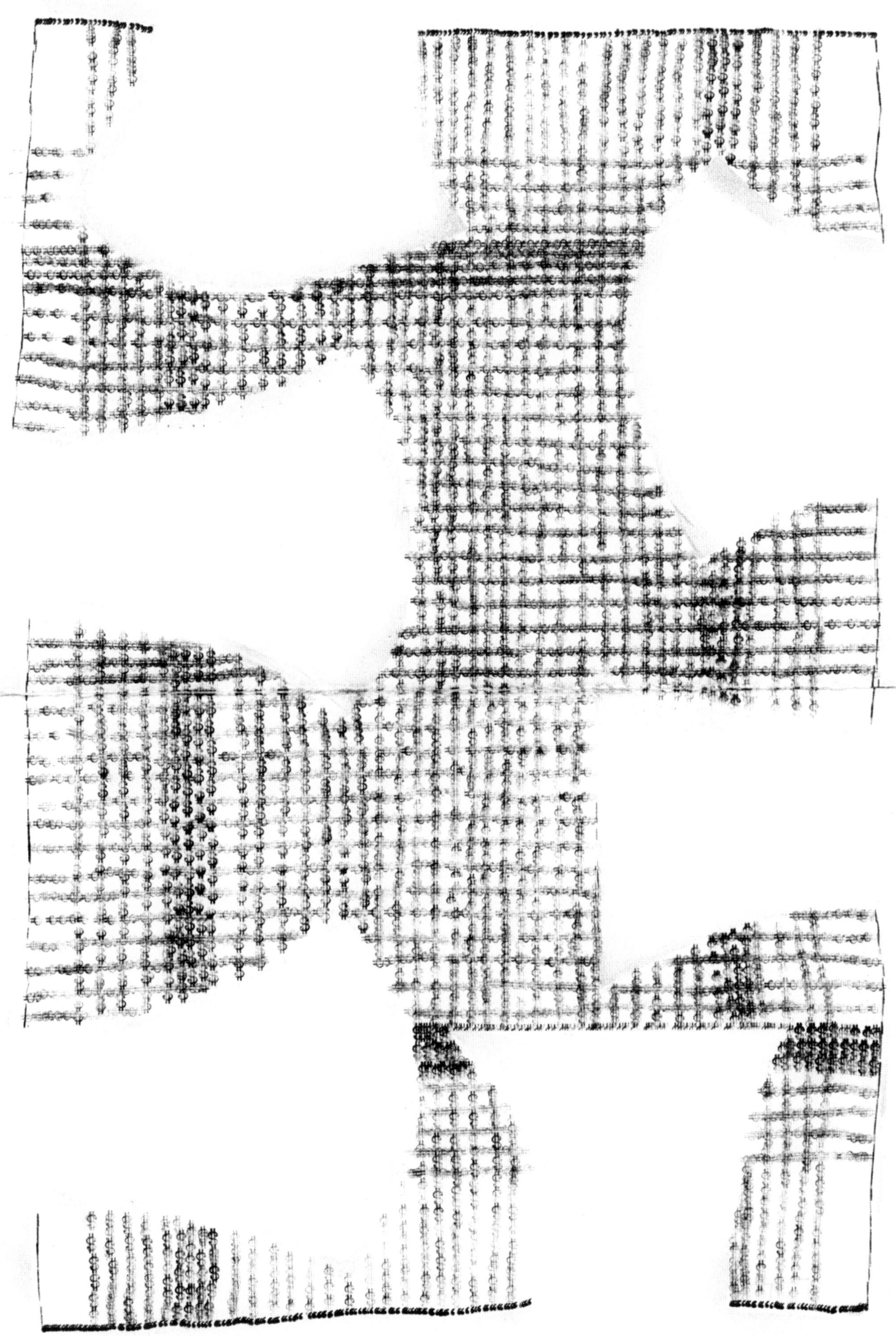

TEA TOWEL CUT UP TO MAKE FACE MASK 10/06/2020

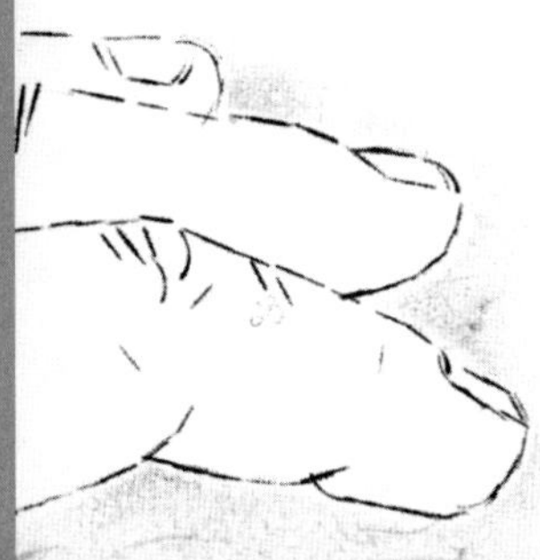

UNTOUCHED FINGERS 10/10/2020

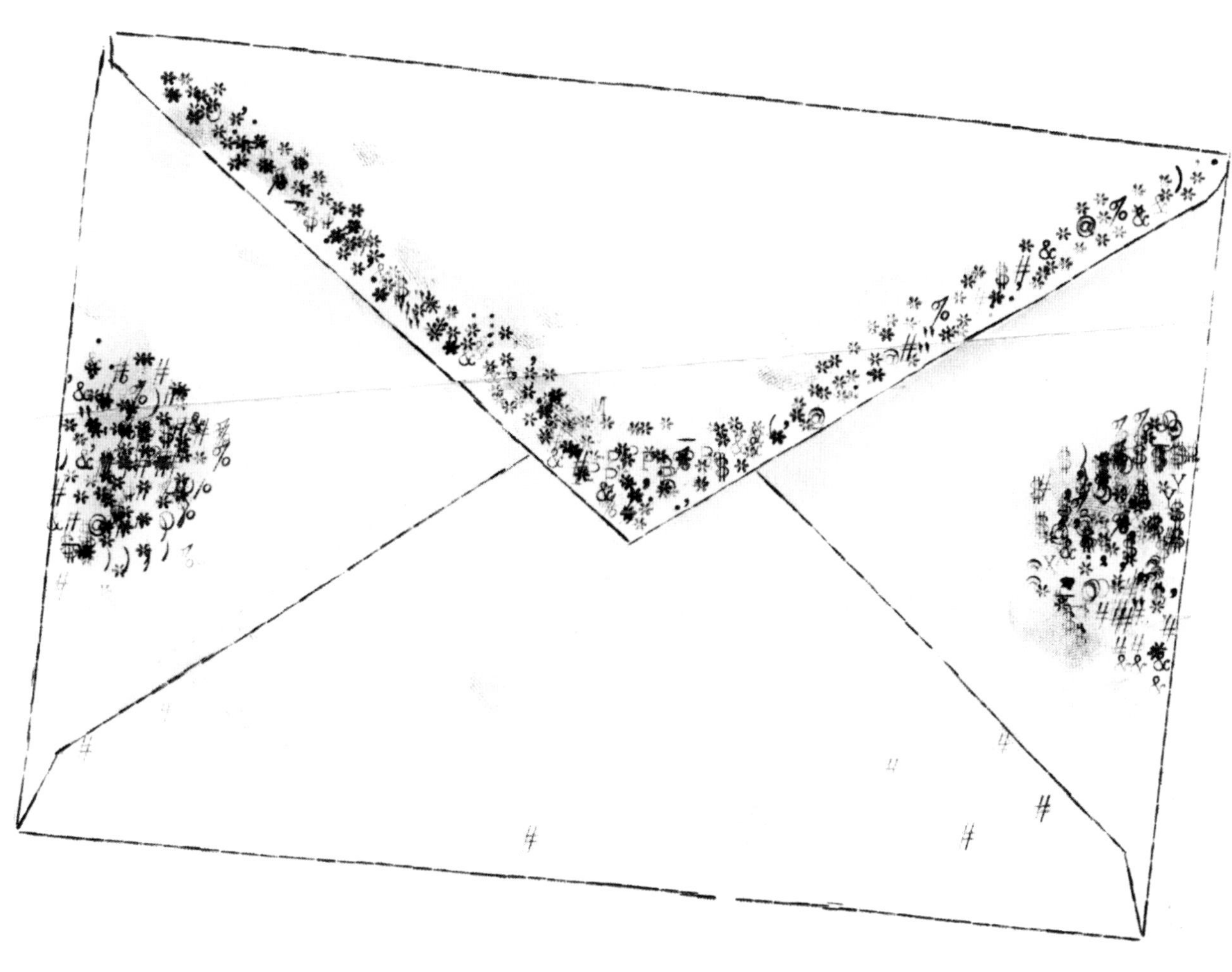

IMAGINED GERMS ON THE MAIL 10/12/2020

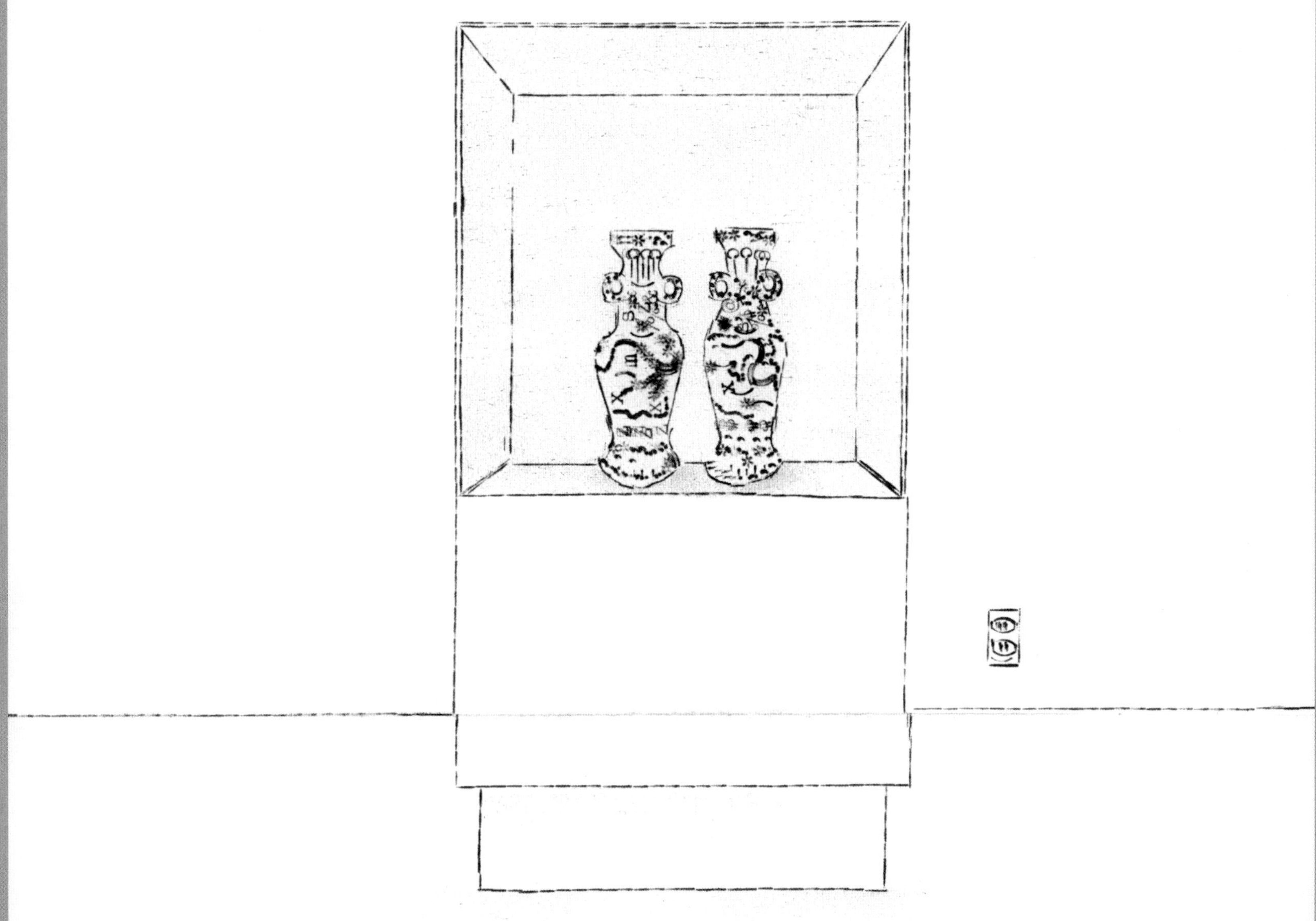

THE SILENT MUSEUM 10/12/2020

NOSTALGIA FOR THE APOCALYPSE 10/17/2020

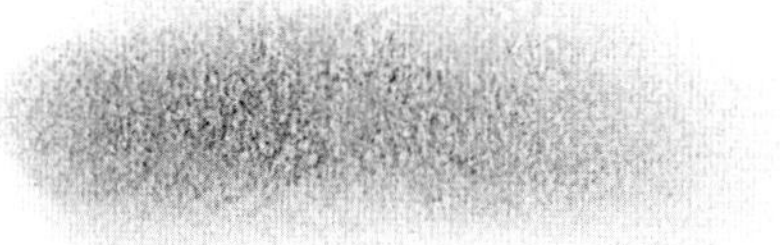

NOSTALGIA FOR THE APOCALYPSE 10/17/2020

T

<u>ABANDONED</u> <u>TO</u> <u>DO</u> <u>LIST</u> <u>10/19/2020</u>

KILLS 99.9% OF VIRUSES* & BACTERIA 10/20/2020

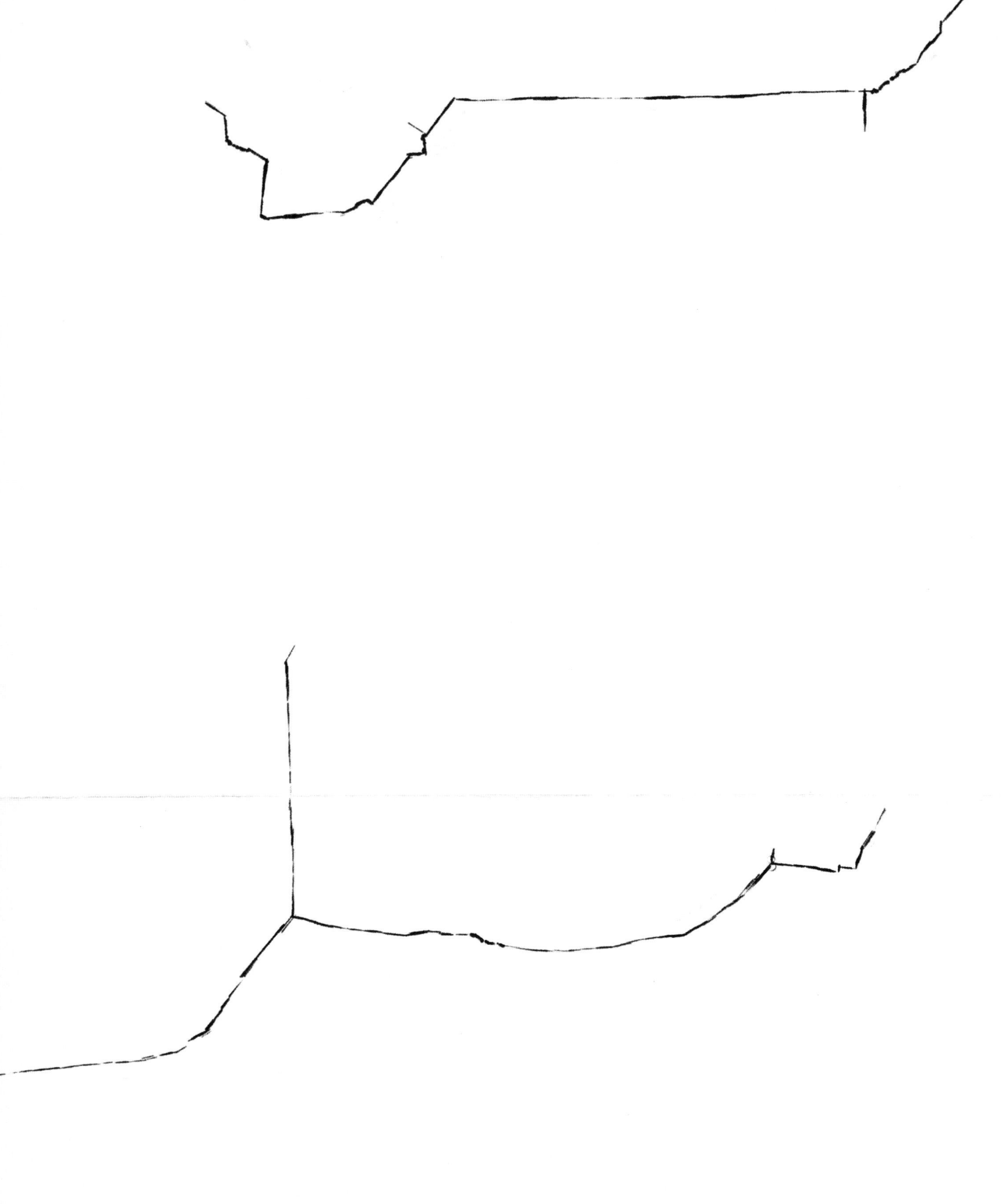

CRACKS IN THE CEILING FROM GYM CLASS IN THE BEDROOM 10/21/2020

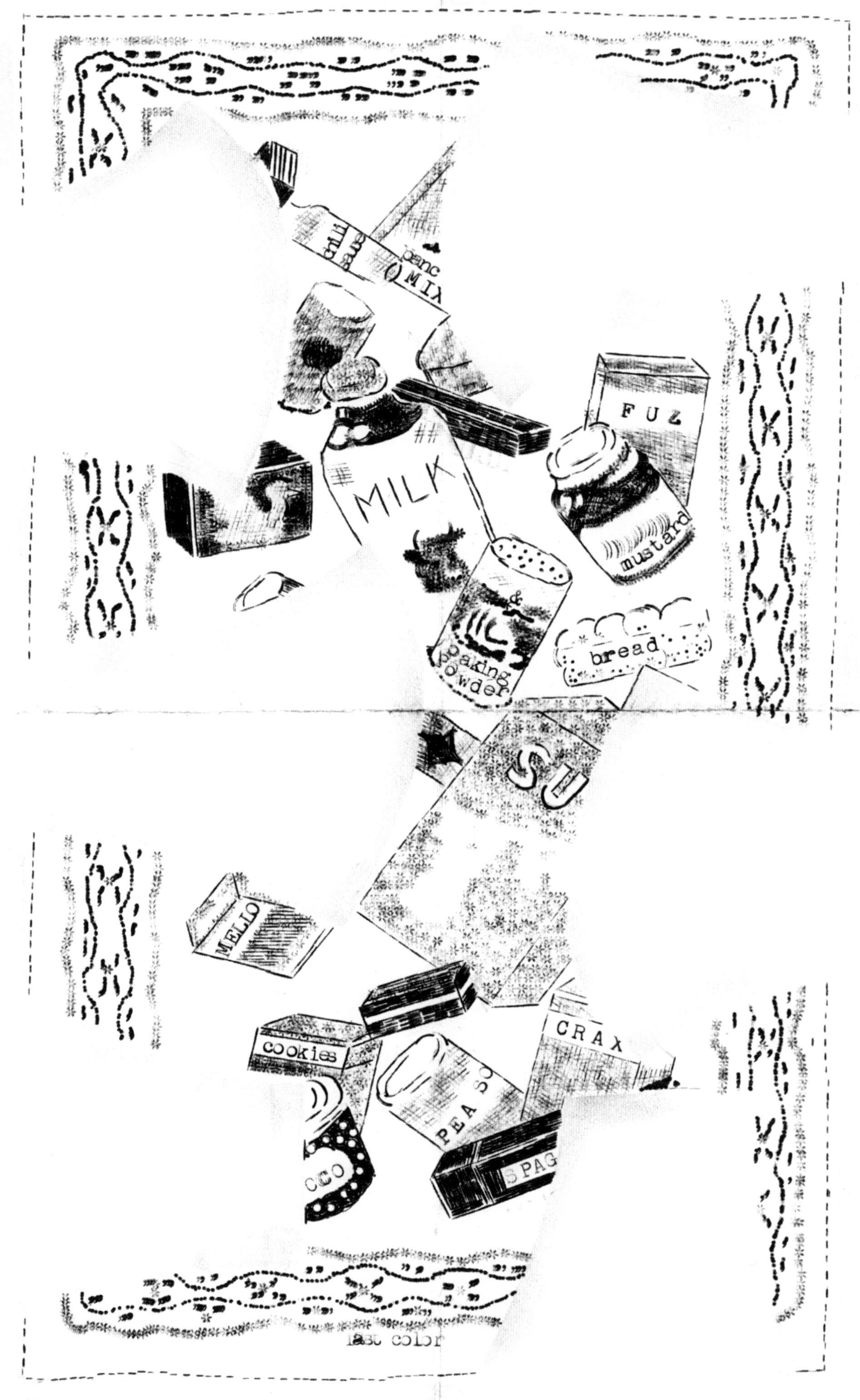

TEA TOWEL CUT UP TO MAKE FACE MASK 10/22/2020

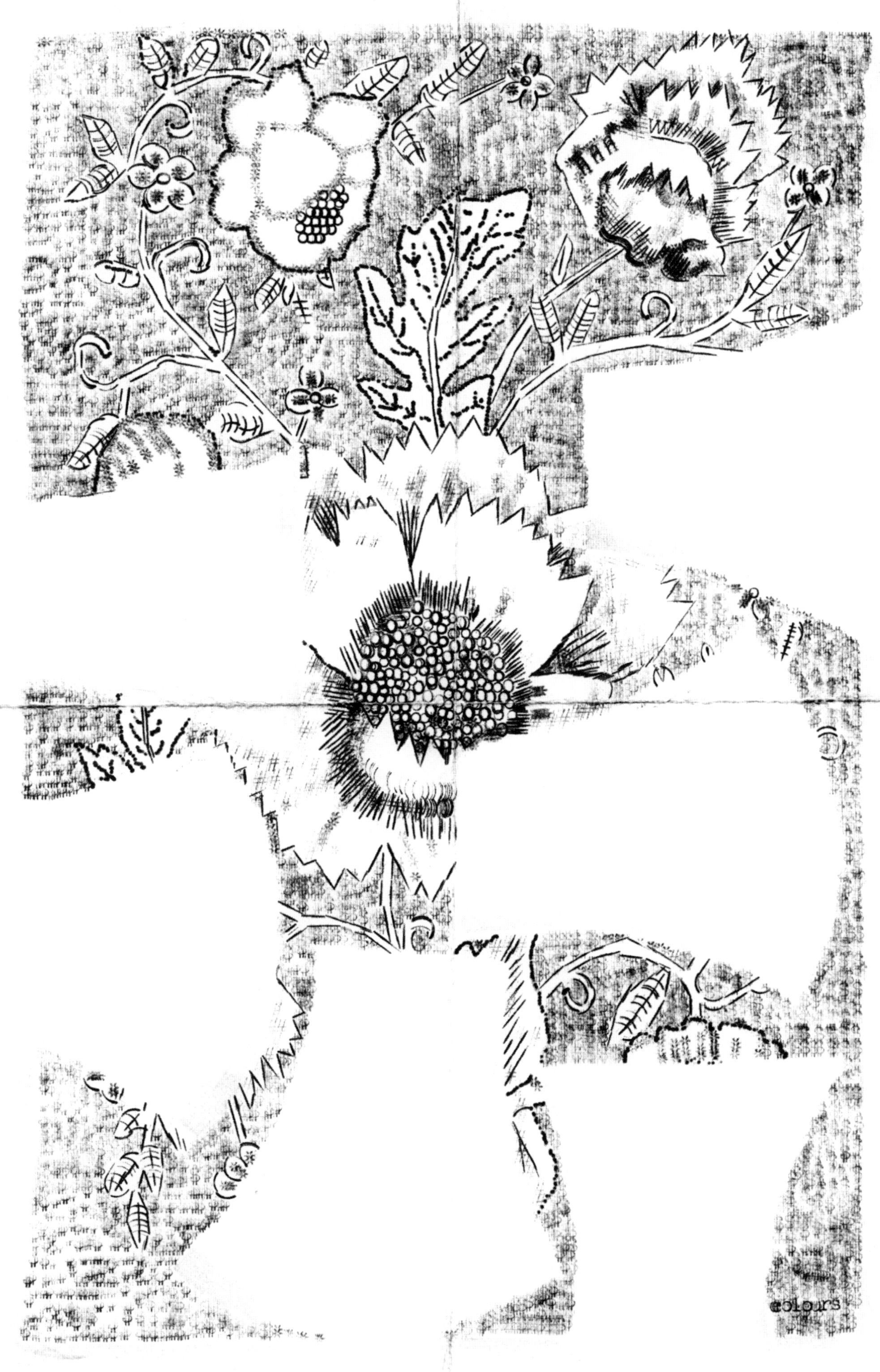

TEA TOWEL CUT UP TO MAKE FACE MASK 10/25/2020

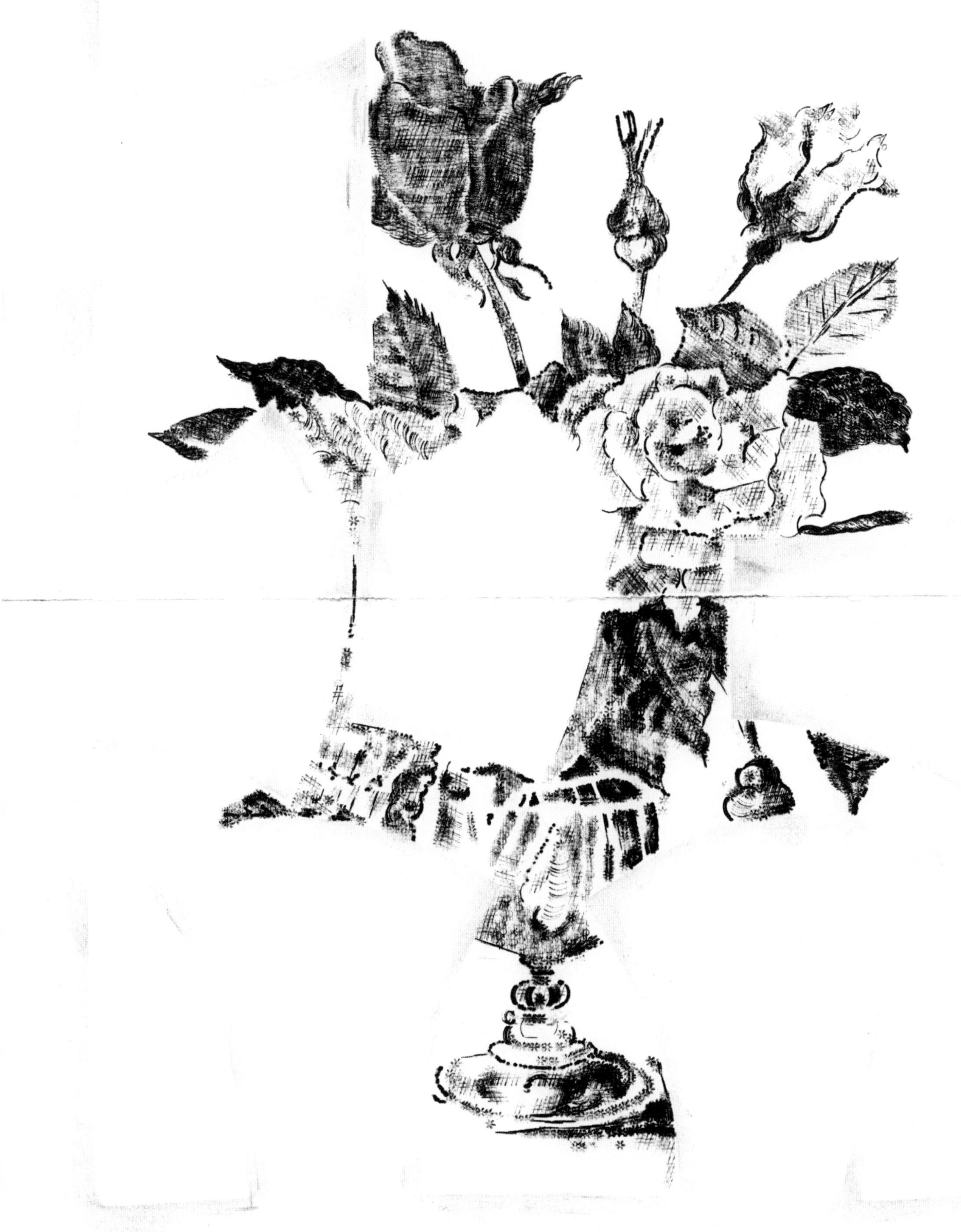

TEA TOWEL CUT UP TO MAKE FACE MASK Io/27/2020

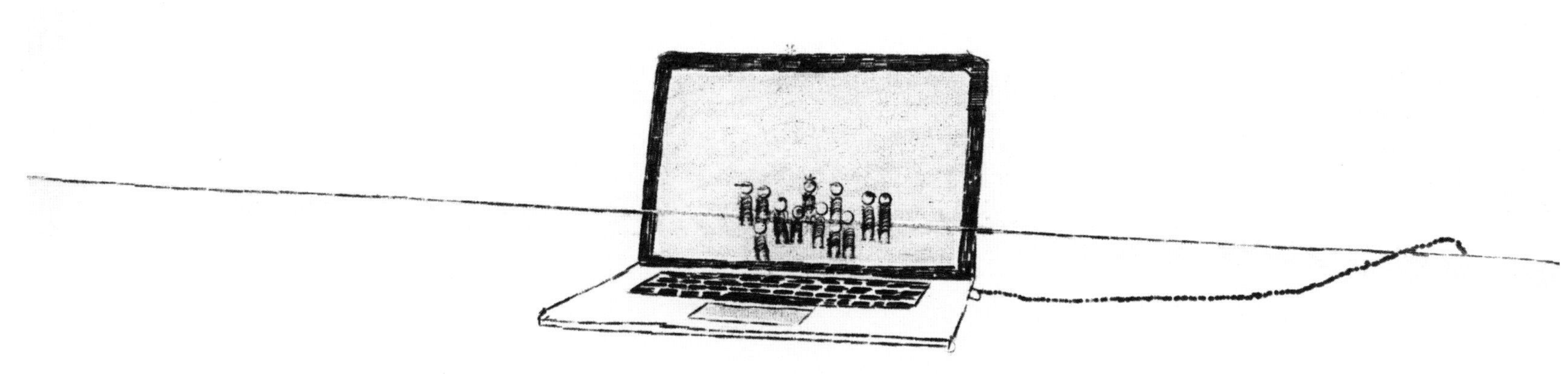

PEOPLE CLOSE TOGETHER 10/27/2020

LENKA CLAYTON

HOW WE THOUGHT IT WOULD BE AND HOW IT WAS.

IMAGES COURTESY OF THE ARTIST AND CATHARINE CLARK GALLERY, SF

FIRST EDITION

ISBN 978-0-9993655-7-I

BOOK DESIGN BY JASON FULFORD

PRINTED IN DENMARK BY NARAYANA PRESS

LENKACLAYTON.COM

JANDLBOOKS.ORG